These Dry Bones

these dry bones

by
E Dot Marie

Copyright © 2011 by Estee Nsek

ISBN: 978-1-7355421-0-2

All rights reserved. No part of this book may be reproduced, scanned, or distributed in any printed or electronic form without permission.

First Edition: June 2011

Second Edition: September 2020

Printed in the United States of America

Cover design by Ashley Byrd
Layout design by Emily Anne Evans

This book is dedicated to the internal unrest of reluctant dreamer. To the person with high functioning depression who pushes through daily. The person who lays down with perseverance and gets up with the flow of life only to be routinely swallowed in your traumas and generational patterns. This book is dedicated to you. If I can manifest this dream after so much has gone wrong in my life – can you believe that something will FINALLY go right for you too?

I pray you find the faith to speak to your own dry bones and allow them to come alive!

This book is also dedicated to my 8th Grade Creative Writing Teacher at Grace Yokely Middle School. You introduced me to poetry in a new way that saved my life.

Where I'm Coming From...

Preface

I've always been a bit awkward – the oddball of every social circle I've encountered. For as long as I can remember, people have made me the bud of their jokes. If it wasn't my hair, it was my butt. If it wasn't my butt, it was my clothes. There was always something that seemed to put me outside of the in-crowd, yet somehow I still had some association with them. I didn't realize that I was merely being picked out to be picked on, for such a time as this. I always recognized there was a lot of potential packed in me, yet somehow over the years, life in the world sapped me dry.

All the things I have encountered have led me to this place I'm in now. The attack from the enemy started early and bad seeds were planted in me young. There were childhood molestation issues, followed by playground ridicule and more molestation. My first kiss on the lips was received from an angry place for the sake of appeasing others. I was pressured into kissing another young boy in my kindergarten class one day after school while playing video games. Even though I did not want to do it, I got tired of being called a baby and felt as if there was something I had to prove. Self-esteem and confidence had to war with everything else being planted in my mind given my experiences. There were many things happening internally with my emotions, where I was angry about the molestation that was occurring, and then blaming myself because it kept happening. I never asked for help because somehow the enemy convinced me it was my fault, but I wanted the issue to go away. While I wanted it gone, part of me grew accustomed to the abuse and felt secure in it. Hanging on to the comfort of the pain was safer in my mind; because I already knew what to expect. The stronghold of perversion altered my perception of life and love which caused my belief system to be twisted. The things I deemed good for me were not healthy relationships, as I gravitated towards older boys who wanted sexual things from me. People wanting sexual favors from me seemed to be a regular thing, so as I grew older, my boundaries for my actual body became less clear, while the real me was locked behind a façade.

Not knowing how to verbally express what was happening with me led me to the pen. There, in my loneliness, a seed was planted. Writing for me was like breathing. I would carry around my notebook and my pen and pour out my over-dramatized teenage afflictions on paper. My ink became the tears that were suppressed behind the smile. Every verse was the silent scream of the angry girl inside my head who was trapped, while on the exterior I diligently worked at being what everyone else wanted me to be. I assumed if I could somehow be the perfect student, it would do away with every negative experience. If I could be the tough girl at school, it would prevent people from trying to take advantage of me like what had been happening at home. I had to put on a tough mask to cover up how scared I truly was. Fear had been rooted deep in my make-up. I decided to include a few selections from this time and take my readers through my journey of self-discovery. Allow them to see where it began and how it has now evolved into a part of me.

I lost the desire to write for a long time, but occasionally I would pick up the pen and be moved to let the words simply flow. There was a period where I could only write to numb the silent depression I was in. As time passed and life kept coming, I gravitated towards other outlets and pushed writing to the back burner of the stove. It was not until I got to college that the urgency of the pen returned to me. As I began to grow in faith, something happened and my writings became different. Yes, I was still writing the pain away, but something about the way I perceived the pain had changed and it caused the words to have new meaning to me. I now understand the power of words. In John 6:63 Jesus said that the words that He speaks are spirit and they are life, and as a follower of Christ my words have that same power. The Lord has given us the power to speak life or to speak death with our words [**Proverbs 18:21**] so, with that understanding, I have an appreciation for the way in which the tone of the meditation of my heart has changed. Each stage in my life produced more for me to write regardless of my understanding of what was going on at the moment. My walk with the Lord became much more serious to me and with that new topics for writing came about.

The title of this collection comes from the 37th chapter of the book of the Prophet Ezekiel. He was sent by the Lord to deal with the rebelliousness of the nation. Here in this chapter, the Lord asks His prophet a very important question... "Can these dry bones live again?" At this point in history the children of Israel, God's chosen ones, had been taken into captivity by the Babylonians. They were in exile and in a broken state as a people. The Lord's wrath had been laid on them for continuously disobeying His command and breaking the covenant. By the time we reach this passage the nation has lost hope and feels as good as dead. Each section of this book ties in with the prophetic experience illustrated in the passage. The experience starts off in a dry place surrounded by dead things, but by the end of the passage, there is an army of living breathing souls brought out of the grave. The Lord commanded his prophet to speak to the bones four times, which is prophetically the number of creation. The Lord created a new thing for his chosen people in this passage from their dead situations and circumstances. They were lacking faith in the very God they vowed to worship.

I have broken this book into seven sections with seven being a representation of completion. It is my desire that these words bring life to someone else who may be lying in disarray in their personal valley of dry bones. Each section of this book is a different stage in life that ventures through my time drifting away from how I was raised, to the pain it caused, and ultimately finding my way back to that narrow path – the road less traveled.

Taken to the Valley consists of poems written as early as the 8th grade. It expresses the tears I never cried from an early childhood molestation issue that festered on the inside. There were sexually immoral seeds planted early through the abuse from a babysitter around age 5 or 6 as well as boys living in the apartment complex I grew up in. I had two Mexican boys molesting me from age 9 until age 11, asking me for sexual favors and feeling on my private parts. It began as something simple like asking to see my bra in the midst of games like hide and seek. The concept of bra-wearing was still new to me at this time, as at the end of fourth grade there was only one other girl who wore a bra. We received a lot of attention from high school boys since we did not look our age. It evolved from simply seeing the bra, to seeing the breast, to eventually touching the breast altogether. I would be told things like, "you don't look your age," "if you didn't look like this I wouldn't have to ask" or, "why did you develop faster than the other girls around me?" The one that really had my mind warped, "if you tell, you will be in trouble so you can't say anything." Things like that caused me to believe that somehow it's because of my body that this type of attention is happening. I didn't want to get in trouble so I just kept my mouth closed. As touching my breast was not enough for his growing sexual urges as puberty set in for him, he began to ask me for oral favors. The threats changed from me getting in trouble if I told, to him physically hurting me if I told. Ironically, the boy who did most of the molesting saved me from an African-American boy in the same complex who attempted to rape me in the bathroom of the apartment as I was home alone. The thing that topped this all off was the fact that he was one of my older brother's friends who was allowed over our apartment all the time. My parents trusted him as did my brother and those are two people whose opinion I trusted. At this point, we have a male babysitter who molested me which my parents trusted, and someone considered a friend who was taking my innocence. This definitely flawed my idea of how men should treat me.

In the midst of boys taking what they wanted from me, girls would want to explore my body. I had a friend whose older brother would have us kiss while wearing animal masks at the age of 8. I can remember as early as the third grade having a "girlfriend" but making sure our secret was hidden from any adults or other kids outside of our circle of girls who all were exploring perverse relationships with each other. Confusion about my sexual preferences frustrated me as a young believer. Though I knew the bible taught me homosexuality was wrong, the thoughts still came, followed by guilt for feeling the way I felt. I then became even more perplexed because it seemed to be socially acceptable for girls to interact that way – just not boys. The media made it cool, as well as the hype about boys loving the whole idea of two girls together. My anger and sorrow built the mountains of guilt from dabbling in the "alternative" lifestyle lying in the valley of my life and I watched myself slowly begin to dry up. Watching the transition from the first poem to the last one in this first section, we see the hurt build up a wall around my heart to the point of inward isolation.

Breathless Bones Move demonstrates a period in my life where I am internally frustrated with who I am. The struggle most teenagers go through in trying to discover who they are was extremely complicated for me because all I wanted was to please everybody. I wanted to make my parents proud. I wanted to fit in with the in-crowd. I wanted to be what everybody thought I was, but I was really just a scared little girl wracking my brain, attempting to figure out a way to satisfy everyone I came across. This is the season in my life when I developed my first layer of masks. I became a different person depending on what group I was around. At home, I was my parents' little angel and at school, I was a teacher's pet. However, there were certain friends that came around which caused me to become the tough girl – the protector. I became this mean mug enforcer who was not afraid to fight with boys. The name I received from my basketball coach after the awards banquet became the alias I was known as for a time – "powerhouse." Switching masks and adding layers on top of layers became redundant and draining. I grew weary of shifting and just wanted to be myself, but I lost which face was truly mine. During this time, I had my period where writing was no longer my therapeutic weapon of choice. There was a large gap between the poems "Solace," which came around the middle of my sophomore year of high school, and "Tomb Raider," which came about after college. I needed something about my routine to change drastically.

Now the section **God Speaks** may seem short, but it didn't take much for God to get my attention. I was raised to know who God was, and my parents did everything they could to instill a great foundation in me. God instructs every believer, "Train up a child in the way [s]he should go: and when [s]he is old, [s]he will not depart from it." [**Prov 22:6**]. So I lost myself in the freedom of college living and the party scene. The hell that had me trapped in my emotions soon became covered with a religious mask. After I left the party scene and ran back to church, it became my new drug of choice. I began hiding from my past in church, running from my testimony. In a sad attempt to undo that which I had done, and prevent myself from going back, I did more outward things in the church house, and I needed a reality check. I tried to earn my way into God's good graces because it was hard for me to understand that his grace and mercy is not something that could be earned. Just like the children of Israel complained the whole time they were in transition from Egypt, the place of bondage, to the Promised Land, liberation; I complained and held on to my pain because it was what I knew. All those deeply rooted seeds caused me not to joyfully accept the journey I had to travel, but rather I criticized it. I hated life internally but I smiled over it because I refused to be viewed as weak or sensitive. Yet, the Lord spoke to me in the midst of my hiding and explained to me that everything I went through had a purpose.

By the time we arrive at **Breath for the Slain**, the dry bones of my life have come together and have the ability to move. However, that religious mask had me simply operating, doing many works for God without God, like a modern-day Pharisee. I knew all the rules: what to say, when to say it, how to say it, when to cry – on cue, etc. I figured out how to use my gifts in the church and thought I could hide behind the gift given to me without staying in a relationship with the gift giver. There was a sense of pride about the change that had taken place – and somewhere in the back of my mind, I thought it was some goodness of my own that was aiding me in my new found walk. This was a serious transitional period in my life- an eye-opener.

I moved out of that religious routine of doing that which I felt obligated to do in order to fulfill my Christian duty, to being in a place where my love and appreciation for God moved me. I truly gained an understanding of what the sacrifice of Jesus meant for me. I realized that it was nothing but HIS grace that kept me from being seriously hurt physically during those years of molestation. I understood it was nothing but his love that protected me from being stabbed when I had a disagreement with another young girl in my apartment complex and we both came outside with knives in our hands. I knew His mercy was real when I had to spend the night in a juvenile detention center only to be sent to a better high school in the district, with no record attached to my name. Everything the devil had tried to make a bad situation in my life, God was using to benefit me just like the word says: All things work together for the good of them that love the Lord and are called according to His purpose [**Romans 8:28**]. I began to fathom all that had really been done for me. He had breathed new life into me.

Live Again is the pinnacle of my life where this book is conceived. The dry bones of my life have come back together and I've gone from a state of existing, to living and dreaming again. My circumstances could not dictate what my outcome would be. A 5 year failed relationship was the catalyst to walking healed from those childhood traumas. There were no professional therapy sessions that fixed my depression. That's not to say there is anything wrong with therapy, or that I would not recommend it – this is just my personal experience. The Holy Spirit met me in my room many nights and gave me some hard truths which opened my perspective. The Lord used his prophets, yes they still exist, to speak life back into me. I believed the word that was prophesied into my valley and that which is written in the word of God. The awakening of that realization caused me to want to live the abundant life promised to believers in John 10:10. I did not want to go through life and not make an impact. I had always wanted to be a positive role model for young black girls with esteem issues growing up. Now I know how powerful words are, so I figured if I could use my words for some good and spread some truth, rather than the façade I always used to put on – life would have meaning again. If I could just let someone know that they too can come out of the depths of depression, where you want to slit your wrists, or pop a whole bottle of painkillers, or just stay in a dark cave where no sunlight can get in – then I will have done my job.

This is my first book which is a testament to my growth in perspective as a child of the Most High. It illustrates my struggles with accepting myself as a young teen, my quest for love, and the ultimate soul searching we all go through as individuals. The book of Revelations states "And they overcame him [the accuser of the brethren] by the blood of the lamb and the word of their testimony." [**Rev 12:11**] This book is my declaration to myself that my hopes and dreams are not dead and gone, but they are yet resurrected and can live again. Moreover, not only a declaration to myself but also to others, who are still broken and trying to find their way out from the dry valley of pain, that they too can live again. There is hope. You can trust again. You can love again. It's all possible with Jesus Christ.

Table of Contents

Where I'm Coming From... vii

Portrait of a Girl (an introduction) 1

Taken to the Valley 5

Breathless Bones Move 19

GOD Speaks 31

Breath for the Slain 39

Live Again 53

Portrait of a Girl
(an introduction)

Open your mind
Come with me on a journey
I want to introduce you to a special little girl
She's a sweet little thing
Got a grown woman shape but she's only 8
And the big boys like her
Grab at her
And the girls talk about her
She doesn't understand why she can't just look like the rest of them
She plays by herself until she finds a friend
She can't protect herself, but she can protect sandy
She doesn't know how to shield herself so she trains herself not to feel
Learns to take the blows
Because her brother taught her that big kids don't cry
Crying is for babies, kids who are weak
So, she numbs herself to feelings and only seeks to protect

                Every year it's the same
                old story
          She doesn't fit in with the kids
            Doesn't have the latest fits
       All she wants is for them to love her
     All she wants is the friendship of another
One that doesn't consist of backstabbing and insults but this is all she sees

She gets home and the love she sees is arguing
Take care of the little one
Take care of her brothers
No time for dolls, time to be a mother

Maybe if she gets involved in activities, then her parents will make time for her
Nope, still too busy sitting at home arguing
Going to the church doing the work of ministry
Chasing dreams of the industry
And she sits at home and wonders *"what about me?"*

She looks at old photos of when her parents met
Sees a wedding picture and thinks - *"was I an accident?"*
When she looks around all she sees is war
But this is what love is
This is what the fighting is for

Daddy isn't around to save her from the mess
Boys hurt her silently but she thinks it's them she must protect
So, she disappears inside her mind somewhere around age 9
Numb to the things she's asked to do
Obedience was beaten into her - so what it's nothing

He wants to see her bra, he wants to see her panties
He's interested in her
or so she believes
No one ever wants to talk to me - she thinks
If it will keep him giving her the attention she wants from
Mom and Dad, she'll do what she has to do

                This makes her feel wrong
             This makes her feel dirty
       He comes to her rescue when the neighbor
          tried to rape her
      He makes her feel dirty
   She knows this is wrong

Inside she screams and cries and wants someone
Anyone to come home
But they don't
Everyone goes on about their business

       Take care of the baby
     Cook for the boys

She gets straight A's in school so everyone thinks she's ok
She looks out at a world that can't see her pain
Because it's masked in achievements and meaningless trophies

       Pain has become her drug
     She likes to play with knives

She's got a grown woman body
Thick lips, nice tits, child-bearing hips
A booty that even made some girls look twice
Her body was nice
The bad boys want her
And she likes the attention
They treat her like crap but in her mind, that is affection
But she couldn't be weak
Not like her mother
So, she starts treating men like toys

Everybody played with her now it's her turn to play
She's been used up and she's gonna do men and women
the same way
She was a sex object for many so she had no respect for her body
She's giving it away to different men teasing different women in a
twisted attempt to get back at the ones who used her up before

A bittersweet romance between girl and pain
But she knows she's wrong so here comes depression and shame
What's left to do now, drink the problems away
But she masks it in the fun and games

                        So high, so high, she can touch the sky
                        She's walking with who she's become on cloud 9
                        So high so high but she can't fly away
                        At the end of the day death seems like the better alternative
                But she's too much of a punk to take her own life
So, she drives while she drinks
        Yet always protected, always makes it home safe
                She sits up one night and she waits

When will the nightmare end
She wants to stop playing pretend
No one knows inside she's already dead

Love tries to find her but comes wrapped in offense
She's trying to see past it but hasn't mastered it yet
She wants to let love in
But the only love she knows hurts
She'd rather be without love than experience the curse
And protect love from herself...

So, imagine a grown woman as that numb little girl
I've just introduced you to myself...

Taken to
the Valley

Beyond the Sunrise
(8th grade)

I look through my window just before dawn
Beyond the sunrise
I see a world of miraculous colors waiting

As I step forward, the colors quickly fade
One by one they vanish without a trace

I make a right at the pinkish light
A new world of colors appears
Pink and Red and Orange too
A new color for every step

Beyond the sunrise
the colors change to faces - some familiar
some of them new

If to look at my life from the faces' view
I realize no one is me but me
Not another person shaped or designed like me
No way you can change it

Just look at yourself from this point of view and
maybe you will see- no geeks, no freaks
just someone unique.

Dresses and Skirts

Society has made its standards of which I choose not to uphold

My spirit can't be bound by all this hate
all this pain and

this CONFORMITY

I am an individual
not like the rest of these robots

I refuse to be the lady-like girl who wears dresses and skirts

I am not the girl who sits quietly to be
physically, emotionally, and mentally scared

I am the girl who speaks my mind
Wears baggy boy clothes when I feel the need

I am the girl who burps at the table
Has a switch when I walk and

Doesn't care what you really think

Things Hidden

You don't want me to know
    But I see things hidden
        Deep down I know
What lies beneath
      You can't hold it forever
        Your guilt eats up your insides
            To the point where you
           want to
          breakdown and cry
    I see things hidden
        That you don't want me to know
      It's too bad how your actions let it show
Don't think you can make it better
      by saying those three little words
          Because if I took them away
      then what would you say
    Your secrets and lies
Kill you inside
        You let on like it's cool
          but I know it's killing you
      You're talking in your sleep
    while you're lying next to me
  I see the things hidden
      No secrets.
No lies.

Clear Vision

If love is such a wonderful thing
why does it hurt so?
If love is meant to bring such joy
why do we cry so?
If love is so many wonderful things
why do we feel such pain?
If it could be real
If it really, could be
why does it never work for me?

Tormented by everyone lost in "love"
I sit and observe the blindness it brings
Friends get dumped
Obligations ignored
Because yes, because we're in love
It's a bunch of s_ _t
I must say I was blinded by it once
But now I see
I can truly see

I feel sorry for those who still believe
But happy that I am no longer blind

My Own

You think you have me
But I am my own
My soul belongs to no man

        I am my own
        Constantly you call
        Try to bring me down
        with the reveries of your
        past outings and such but
        I keep my cool

                You can't bring me down
                You can try to wrap me
                around your finger
                That finger that has
                explored all the essence
                That is woman but never
                No never has it touched my
                own

        Because I am my own
        It belongs to me
        My heart is no man's
        My soul
        My every being
        It all belongs to me

Life's Cycle

Life is like the sun that rises
Always there and taken for granted
It's the river that flows into the great oceans of the land
The wind that blows making a summer breeze

        The flowers that bloom in the spring
        First planted and then waited upon for the proper season to come
            Nourished to a thing of beauty
                Then one day reached full potential
                      Bloomed into a great creation
                Soon after wilted and withered as time takes its toll
                The thing of beauty becomes weak and weary

Life is a cycle that begins and ends
Life leads to death....

Untitled no. 1

The sky is an unending place

    No beginning

        No end

            Just an open space

My heart is like that void up there

    No beginning

        No end

            No heat

    No air

        I just feel for you

            In that quantitative amount

Solace

Solace
Never to be found
Consumed by this emptiness

                              Surrounded by a dark, black void
    Sorrow
        Heartache
            Anger
                Sadness

Spinning in the madness around
Thoughts run wild

    Searching
        Hoping

Trying to understand

                Why?
        Why?
Why…

Still searching in the darkness
Trying to find that small tunnel of light

Silent Pain

I could shed a thousand tears

    that would not even begin to express

        the pain I feel

            Suffering many afflictions

                The knives stab deep

                    Not of the enemy

                Instead of the bitter irony

            which is mind boggling

        Too insane to comprehend

    How could one who loves me so

cut a wound so deep?

Death

I used to know how to love once
Some time ago
But now my heart is hard and cold
Sometimes I think I have no soul

        So much anger and pain locked away
      Deep inside my heart
   I don't think I could find love in me if I tried
I wouldn't know where to start

        I could not take it anymore
        All the heartache
        So, I've learned to exist without the sensation
        Just loneliness and rage

Sometimes I wish I could end it all
    It's not like anyone would care
        When I was going through real tough times
          Not a soul was there

I've shut out all those thoughts
that slightly connects to love
That way not a soul can get too close
It won't happen again
All the love in my heart has finally come to an end

Breathless Bones Move

Quiet Storm

Hi.
My name is Estee.
I'm emotionally numb.
I don't trust anyone.
Sometimes I feel like screaming,
but nothing ever comes out.
All I want is to be ok.

Hi.
My name is Estee.
My innocence was taken from me.
Since then I've always felt a bit strange.
The ones closest to me
cut the deepest wounds I have.
And they don't let them heal,
They keep cutting...
But the blood doesn't show
internally I bleed.

Hi.
My name is Estee.
All I feel is pain.

Hi.
My name is Estee.
Inside my tears fall like rain.

Inside

Every day is a mystery
My entire life is making me go crazy
I need a change from the scenery

Anywhere but here seems like a good idea
Which path to take
The decision seems scary

What if it leads me to a place I don't want or need to be?

Inside I'm slowly dying
I'm crying inside

I'm breaking down because of this life
and the way everybody wants me to be
But I can't be anyone one by me

I'm still trying to figure out
who me really is...

Untitled no. 2

A thousand needles poke my eye
This is the pain I feel as I say goodbye
I never meant to hurt you
I never meant to make you cry
I wanted to love you

Honestly, I tried
but you wanted more than I could give you
For this I am sorry
But what can I do?

All I have I gave
but it wasn't good enough to sustain you
To bring you pain makes my heart ache
But this is what I must do

Trust me
It's better this way
I must leave you

Untitled no. 3

My life is painted in shades of black and grey
Depressing
Yet, exciting
All at the same time
You do not understand
but I did not expect you to
Just know my life would not be what it is without you

I hurt so bad from day to day
It seems like there is nothing
to subdue the pain
Someone once told me
"hold on... pray..."
Some how
Some way
I will make it through this rain

Spread Wings

Why must you constantly tell me lies?
These lies you tell bring tears to my eyes
A constant affliction you inflict on my being
Every time you say these lies to me

Like a burning arrow
Piercing my heart
It is hard to tell your truth and your lies apart
Truth vaguely shines through those lips
Mostly it is your conniving lying
and your quick wits

I hate the fact that you can seem so sincere
But no longer will I stay cooped up here
All the lying stops today
because I've found the strength to
spread my wings and fly away

Lovely Wounds of the World

I've thought long and hard
of what is and what was
I've realized it was all pointless

Love, it's time we had a talk
Why do you torment me so?
You keep playing games with
my mind
I don't know how much more I
can take
You lead me on with every
excuse you make
You've shattered my heart in
every place
There is no ounce left to save
The damage is done
The toll has been paid

Love, leave me alone
I don't want to play these
foolish games
They've been tearing me apart
They've broken me apart
I'm frozen cold
I'm wounded deep
Nothing of this world
Could ever bring heat
There is no heat warm enough
To heat this block inside my
chest

There is no more beat
The rhythm died

Love, I admit defeat
You've had your fun
My time has come
I am done

The Light

In the darkness of the room
This cold dark room
shined a light so faithful and true
All through the night it shined
During the yelling, the crying, and
even the silence...
It shined.

This light has opened my eyes
to a bigger picture
This shining light never failed once
to keep its crimson shine
It just shines on for me
In the silence, the light just smiled
Through the crying and yelling
the light sang a song of comfort to me

This light shined through the
deep
dark
night
Hungry, dirty and ashamed I sat
And still the light shined on
Afraid, shivering and cold I lay
And still the light shined on

Shine light shine
Keep on shining
For the shimmer you give is
The peaceful luster of reassurance
Shine light shine

Tomb Raider

Hidden in the tomb
Way deep in the darkness,
Dying to come out when the Tomb Raider comes

The deeper you dig, the more support is needed
Without it runs the risk of what surrounds caving in
Then we'll all be locked in, buried deep in the tomb

The light is shut out
The panic sets in
Followed by a gust of fear…
And the breeze of doubt…

The great escape…
Set me free!

You cannot resurrect what's already full of life

The Tomb Raider seeks out the treasures lost
hidden in a place of death

GOD Speaks

Silence

Why is the silence so unbearable?

Is it because in the silence YOU are speaking
It has become deafening
Some would rather have their ears bleed
than to sit still in the silence of YOUR speech

But I want to hear from YOU
Resist the temptation to turn on the TV
Allow the music to stop playing
Listen to the thickness of the silence
while YOUR peaceful breath of life touches my face

In the silence
YOU are speaking
I'm fighting my flesh
Trying to listen

In the silence
I lay and listen...

Self Esteem

I just want to feel like I'm somewhere I belong

Didn't you know you were fearfully and wonderfully made?
I never intended you to be like the rest
I created you for my purpose and will
In my eyes, you are my earthly treasure
As rare as a pearl from the depths of the sea

But when I look in the mirror that's not what I see
I don't see jewels, I see dust
Nothing on this cursed earth but crust
I know all I do is fuss
But Lord it's a must
Make me love what I see
When my reflection looks back at me

When you begin to understand
that I hold you in the palm of my hand
I formed you in my image and likeness
When you seek and find me
that is when you will see
exactly who I created you to be

Hush

Hush little Christian don't you cry
Sin that besets you has to die
You prayed so long for help to come
Now that it's here, why you trying to run

If you just know who you are in me
You'd see the truth shall set you free
No hurt, harm, or danger can come to you
Don't be scared to do what I called you to

Lay hands, heal the sick, and prophesy
Move mountains, change lives, and yourself deny
Know me in the fellowship of suffering
With that comes life and life more abundantly

Gifts

The gift is NOT the ministry
yet ministry is a gift
But when it becomes about you
and that flicker of pride gets kindled
remember the gift comes without repentance
So, don't assume that you're in good standing
Man looks at the outward appearance
but it's the condition of your heart that I need
Even the pagans who didn't believe
dropped their gifts at Jesus feet

and worshipped Him

Operation doesn't equal relationship
You can keep doing the works of God
without the time spent
it becomes nothing more than community service
is it worth it?

The gift giver should never take a back seat
to something so temporal
It's the giver of the gift you need
What will you have if that talent is taken back
If the very thing you used to identify you
is snatched up
voice silenced
legs weak
pen… no ink

Come back to your first love
Your original gift was me
The salvation of my only son's blood
is the best gift you could receive
But you treat it like manna because
you know not what it means
But in the midst of your complaining,
I still supply your every need

You prostitute the anointing to
satisfy your greed
then try to stamp my name on it
But my seal of approval – never released
You're so puffed up with that original sin
But take head to this warning because you
know what happened to him

Consecrate your gift my child
Set it aside for me
Only then can all that "faith" send
a sweet-smelling aroma to me

Scars

Your scars are where your true beauty lies
You try to mask them behind this false sense of bliss
Your smile is remiss for a place far off in another dimension
You dress it up nicely and deserve an Oscar nomination
The way you hold it down is just that good

Yet in the midst of the smiles, your light is running out
The battery has lost its charge
That tiny flame of *the real you* begins to shine its way through
Don't put out your beacon of light

The ugliness you faced in your life
is the essence of the beauty that shines in your eyes
Every tear that you have cried cleansed them
and washed the dirt away

Your scars make you beautiful
They make up a piece of you
Every scar holds a story of another victory
You have overcome

Breath for the Slain

New Years Thoughts

2008
The year of new beginnings
The only thing that seemed to begin was
a new level of self doubt and frustration

New hurts
Unexpected pains and
at the end of the year there was
a new change
a push
a shift
to take me out of what seemed so comfortable

A new way of thinking
A new way of living
Like a caterpillar ready to go to the cocoon
The transition in living life is knowing
I'm meant to turn into something beautiful
Spending my days
Waiting for the change

A safe location needs to be found
to allow the transformation
to take place

Towards the end of the year of new beginnings
I've been lead to a new place
a new way of seeing
a new level of worship
a new place to call home
Now I enter 2009 -
The year of Divine completeness in the Lord
The year to produce fruits
The year to begin building the cocoon
The time has come for a transformation

My life has been a buildup in anticipation
of becoming a butterfly
Time to begin the process
For without the process beginning
I'll never know the true vision of
the beauty God intended me to be

What will I look like?
What intricate design will be on my wings?
When the process is finished
We will all see…

Newness

Pain.
This is something I know.
Know it so well that it's comfortable.

Healing.
Something I longed for.
Yet now that it's in my face,
I'm unsure.

Joy.
Lasts longer than happiness ever can.
Something the enemy comes to steal.

Pain.
The one thing I'm used to.
My safe place.

Healing.

Now it's here
I'm shying away from it.
To step out of 13 years of one thing
into this new thing is scary.

Fear.
Not of God.
Get over yourself, Estee.

Pain.
Healing.
Fear.
New.

New.

New.

New.

Estee's Lament

Have you ever been surrounded by love,
yet felt it didn't touch you?
All you wanted was a look
a touch
a smile
a feeling
but when you look around the room
looking for that special contact
all you feel is more alone
and now more than ever need someone to hold
yet no one will do
all you have left is you

Everything I have to offer
not many can receive
but what I have to give doesn't come from me
So, I stay alone
and that's when God comes
and he dries my tears
and I no longer have to fear
because he'll take the pain away
He'll give me a brand-new day

He'll make me believe that
someone could truly love
a wretch like me
All my faults
All my mess
Every single part of me
Every mistake
Every crazy thought
The parts that make up me
He knew before he made me
Every spot I'd hold
I was never meant to fit into the mold
The crowd that everyone wants to put me in
I can't fit in
It was never his intent
So I wait on him to draw me in
And make me believe
Until then I'll just lament

Mustard Seed

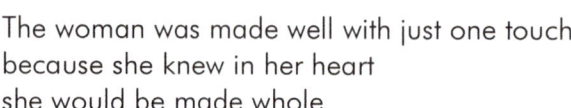

If all it takes is the faith of a
mustard seed,
does this mean that I really
don't believe?

The woman was made well with just one touch
because she knew in her heart
she would be made whole

But when I pray
I think I believe
Yet the enemy must be laughing at me

It seems the pain is more intense
Now I'm almost crying
This doesn't make sense

I know it takes a mustard seed to move a mountain
How much lack is in me?
That pain in my body refuses to leave

Without faith, it's impossible to please Him
Without faith, it's impossible to win

Enemies

Everyone has enemies
But I have found that my biggest enemy is me

The inner me
The me that no one else can see
The me that talks me out of things
The me that doesn't like what she sees

The me that tears me down
Before anyone else can
The me who convinces me
No one else understands

People will always have enemies
But I don't worry about them
My worst enemy
Is the inner me
The me that can't accept love from anyone

The spirit is willing
but the flesh is weak
The inner me beings to speak

Most people have enemies
My biggest enemy
is the inner me
Constantly trying to self destruct

A lot of people have enemies
My worst enemy
Is the inner me

Prophet's Cry

What exactly am I supposed to say
The words I use are taken lightly
When I open my mouth it's like a joke
So, what more do you want
I have no more words to express
What this is
I have no more tears
I have nothing
There is nothing left here
Nothing left inside
What more can I say?
What more can I do?
It grieves me when I look at you
It pains me to see what we have become
Yet such is the cup that I must drink from
Such is the pain I must endure
Such is the hand that was dealt to me
This is what I signed up for

Peace Be Still

I know that I can do all things through Christ
The Lord never gives me more than I can bear
But this pain
This storm
is slowly eating me up inside
The winds are blowing
It's growing cold
I know trials come to build faith
And this is supposed to cause me to grow
But how can I grow if I'm drowning?

A seed drenched in water dies
Lord, this rain is killing me
I have no words left

The storms in my life have me so cold
I'm numb
While all things are supposed to work together
for my good
I can't see through this rain
All I hear is thunder
Nothing makes sense

Peace…
Be still

A Brief Moment with God in the Rain

Rain on me…

I yearn for it
I reach out for you in desperation
like a nomad who's been wandering the desert
in search of an oasis

I don't need an umbrella to shield me from this rain
I want to be drenched from head to toe
Covered in your Spirit

I watch the rain…

You are the rain…

I want to take a walk in the rain…

I Gave It All Up

The toxicity had me lost in myself
I had no idea loving him
was so hazardous
The more I tried to make it work
those demons had more room to work
on me
in me
A cancer was spreading
My vision was obstructed
My heart constructed
Walls
I barricaded myself in
Never realized what I was hiding from
was already inside
But in a moment of clarity
When I was positive I would no longer survive the negative
environment in my mind
I gave it all up
and found inner peace
self-worth
I found real love

Live Again

My Letter to Fear

Dear Fear,

I have long awaited this moment when
I can once and forevermore
kiss you goodbye

We've been together so long
everyone could agree
we just meshed together so perfectly
like white on rice, you were my everything

Farewell to your grip on my tongue.
I'm done with the bitter taste you leave
I'm through with the lies you feed me.
I can no longer sit still while you hold me down
magnifying False Evidence Appearing Real

Today I can finally push you off,
shake loose from your hold.
Even when I let go, you held me tight
whispering worry in my ear
Doubt had me dumb

The sour stench you surrounded me with has been fanned away
The realm of "what if" no longer bothers me
The unknown has now become my playground

The unseen is no longer a threat to me
because I know
to whom I belong.
You did not come from the giver of my gifts
So will I keep you - I dare not.
I found the receipt and I'm sending you back
You know you really cramp my style

You never fit me well and your color's very bland
I stood flat foot for you
You had me fooled
Had a firm grip on my hands

But this is my goodbye to you
Farwell
So long

Can't say that I'll miss you
I've been given something much better than you
What I have causes obstacles to move
I can speak to the mountain and watch it change
With the use of the name above every other on this earth
demons will leave and I can have peace

What I have takes me to limitless heights
It is the very essence of the unseen that you tried to talk me out of
This new thing helps me to
Face Everything And Recover
It reminds me of who my father is and all his promises
Full Assurance In The Holy One
FAITH

Thank you so much for showing me how much I doubted God
But my mindset has been changed
I trust what He said and in my belief is where we finally part

Journey

This life is a journey
A journey back to who I am
I knew when I was a child
but somewhere along the way I lost myself
And from about age 9 until now
I've been trying to see if I could meet myself
Reacquaint myself with me
and when I find myself, I can answer
all my questions about me
But I was walking down all the wrong paths
searching for myself
when I never went anywhere
This game of hide and seek seemed endless
but I know where I am now
and I'm on a journey to meet myself

The me I've been searching for
went and stood by her big brother Jesus
and they've been calling me
trying to get my attention
attempting to bring me back

The closer I get to Jesus,
the closer I get to myself
I'm on a lifelong journey
to myself in Christ Jesus...

Therapy

I was numb
to the point where afflicting myself
was an amusing pastime to explore
the levels of pain I could take
I was so miserable I had to make myself break
I submitted myself to Christ Jesus
and gained back some feeling when he took over
my life

I started my physical therapy treatments
to get my feeling back to normal
and I realized this process doesn't
always feel good
but i was prescribed to receive treatment
with you for the rest of my days
until forever comes
and you aid in taking the numbness away
with every session I gain more feeling
my senses are more keen
my sensors awakened

The more I feel you
the more I feel me
You are the best treatment for me
And there is no other therapy I'd rather receive

Corrective Eye Surgery
(response to Clear Vision)

Amazing grace
How you blessed me
I thought I could see but my vision was not 20/20
In ignorance, I felt as though I was free
because I managed to isolate myself
while perception whispered sweet nothings in my ear

And I listened
I savored every word
Became a love hater who had no idea what love was
Angry at the truth because I was stuck in a lie
Convinced that I didn't deserve affection
Accepting the deception of independence
Love tried to help me but my thinking had me believe love was responsible for my pain

I watched what should have been love not work for others
This further fed my perception
Now I realize the scales were simply growing calluses over my eyes
Since I refused to accept the truth
I was getting closer to a reprobate mind
And a strong delusion spoke to me most of the time
But the spirit of God Almighty has used that two edge sword to remove the scales
Love's truth I can recognize

Love won't always give you what you want, but
love always gives you what you need
I was trying to be a spoiled little brat and it caused me not to receive
But thanks to Jesus for his love that saved me
His love is not full of jealousy and control

His love meets the need of the heart that is willing to be free
Now I can choose to stay bound or
believe what was done on Calvary
He came that I could have life more abundantly
He said whosoever believes will have Him in eternity
His father is Love who sent him and this truth made me free
Every lash that slashed his back was an incision to my cornea
The blood that flowed washed every particle of perception from my optic nerve

Amazing grace
How you blessed me
I once was blind but now I see

Cornerstone

The stone that the builders refused
has now become the chief cornerstone...

Access denied
Constantly rejected
From kindergarten until age 23
I've been the butt of everyone's jokes
The one ridiculed and scorned
The one whose name was constantly dragged through mud
And yes, my favorite line to hear
"You're the realist female I know" or better yet
"You're so dope, you're like a sister to me"
Everyone smiled in my face while secretly
they mocked me
Giving hugs and kisses while practicing their black magic
In an attempt to keep me down

The stone that the builders refused...

I had to experience these things to become
Hard as a rock
How can the builder use a weak foundation?
The building would not withstand a great storm
God allowed such a life because he bought me with a price
And no servant is greater than the master
He did rise with all power in his hand but
Let us remember he suffered death to arise

Death to his own will
He gave up the ghost
So that I could freely live in the will of the father
He chose me to be him - a modern day Christ
Christ simply means anointed one and I'm to be that for Him
But before the reject could be turned to the chief

I had to be persecuted and scorned
Willingly suffer myself unto death
Press towards Golgotha without making a gall request
I believe I understand just a little bit
What it felt like to be like Christ
What his heart felt like each time his loved ones steadily denied
Or called him crazy, claimed he was possessed
Tried to trap him tried to frame him
Tried to stone him to death

But the stone that the builders refused has now become
the chief cornerstone...

All my life's experiences have shaped me for the better
Pushed me closer to the father
Made my love for Jesus stronger
I may be the only Jesus someone ever sees
And if that is the case my own must reject me
For it's no longer I who live but the Christ that dwells in me
It's not me you reject but
the one who can set your soul free

The stone that the builders refused has now become
the chief corner stone

Bondservant to the King
(response to My Own)

Emotionalism takes a backseat while
truth remains unchanged
My soul belongs to no man
but I would be lying if I said I belong to myself
My life is not my own because
I'm indebted to a king
He suffered many things
in exchange
I would live under then hand of the I AM who sent He

The prince of the power of the air deceived man out of his rule
But there was a man that came and took that power from his hand
He crucified his desires so I wouldn't have to die
Got beaten unrecognizable so I could be let into the secret place
Every mistake I made has been covered by the grace of his bloodshed
He took on my punishment so that I would live the live he led
I owe Him everything because he gave His life for me
I'm no longer a slave to the sin I was born in
My soul has been redeemed
I'm now a bondservant to a master who is willing to serve me

These Dry Bones

I've dwelt in the valley
where the broken dreams go
Where shattered hearts and dim visions congregate
after they've been snatched away
A desolate land full of disappointment and shame

Depression runs rampant in these parts

I was dragged to that place years ago
when joy was stolen from my soul
Torment prevailed and bitterness reared her ugly head
I've been through the valley of the shadow of death
it was dark and desolate
I felt alone and afraid
in a dry barren place where lifeless bones lay
and the light barely creeps in

Destined to an eternity of pain
I was convinced the Lord did not know my name
Then a still, small voice came knocking at my heart
Yet fear gripped me and I fled to the darker parts
of the valley in the cave
Holding up blinders
Feeding the lies ministering to my mind
Hardening my heart while still having an inward cry

I heard a voice in the darkness singing
You can live again
It was a sweet melodic tune that burst through the airwaves

And beat my eardrum with a rhythm that brought me from my knees to my feet

Come with me says the Lord
I have much to show you
See how you got yourself into this cave
See how every step of the way I knew your name
See how I would not let you die
I allow you to become dry so you will thirst for me
I allow you to lose your sight so you can truly see

If you live for yourself, you cannot live for me
Retrace your steps prior to the valley
It was all about you and your selfish gain
It was all about you
You brought no glory to my name
You mocked me in churches
Tried to claim we were of the same spirit

But my spirit knows of all things
In ignorance, you move and have your being
Surviving off impulse, you try to create your life
Basing it off the prince of this world's lies
And with every plan I was not acknowledged
You mapped your way straight to this valley of death
Where my presence has left and you are dry and desolate
Yet you are my word which cannot return to me void
What I sent you to accomplish will unfold before your eyes
Speak what is in you that I placed deep inside

Gather up your dreams and to yourself prophesy
Power of life lies in your tongue
Resurrecting power given from the Lord God Almighty above
That which I created you to be will be
Speak to this valley and live your life for me
Now that fear has no longer gripped you
Now that bitterness is gone
Now that unforgiving nature has silenced its roar
Give me what I gave you
It's withdraw time
Put out what's put in you

Speak to the valley
Don't let your bones wither and die
Out of your belly flows rivers of life
Speak to the dreams
Call them back from the dream snatcher
Humble your heart to trust that I have you
In your faith, your bones will live again
In your obedience, you will win

I've dwelt in the valley where broken dreams die
Now I'm coming out of the whirlwind saturated in life

The Other Day

What a difference a day makes

Just the other day I was rocking *get em girl* dresses
Hoping to gain the attention of men I never wanted to settle down with

Just the other day I thought relationships were for suckers
I wasn't going to let no man sweet talk me into his
WEB OF LIES

What a difference a day makes
Today I know my value is not found in the assets I've been physically blessed with

Today I understand loving a man is not weakness
On the contrary
it takes much strength
Like that of ants
Who carry over quadruple their body weight

Love is big
Love is heavy
Love is transformational

Word Manifested

In the beginning was the word
And in the end, it shall be
If the Lord stopped speaking for you
though you constantly ignore,
there would be nothing left and your life would end

Your tongue has power
yet you've been fooled to speak death
Singing curses and lies in your ignorant bliss
But my words have power because I have been sent
with the authority of the Almighty
I speak life this day
I have one word for you
and that word is…
Change

Don't accept defeat
All hope is not gone
Come together, write it out
Your victory song
Life is returning
As your new words manifest

The Mirror

Have you ever taken a good look at yourself?
I mean passed the reflection
Have you ever really looked at you?

I looked at myself today
And there was more than just a face
There were the broken dreams of little girls
who have been touched inappropriately by their older brother's friends
There was the self esteem
of the chocolate girls who grew up with the nappy hair
feeling like they needed to wear it straight to *maybe* be beautiful
There were the eyes of women who feared vulnerability because
to give another person access to hurt them again seemed like insanity

I wanted to look away
But I stood in the bathroom mirror
and stared at the dry bones of a nation of women who refuse
to allow old hurts and old fears to drive the car heading to their future
I saw the millions of women being healed by the love of the Father
Being restored to who we were created to be
Cultivators capturing vision and creating beautiful masterpieces on life's canvas
Have you ever stopped to take a look at yourself in the mirror...?
Please tell me what you see...

Untitled no. 4

Beware of the wolves
She was aware he was a wolf
Which is why that silver ring must have burned

But this moment
She was freed

Those words gave her wings
She went flying towards
Abandoned dreams

The silence in the room was deafening
He couldn't believe it was she who found courage to leave
She was done
There's no turning back now

Out the door to new possibilities

She said her final words and left

And the new chapter begins at the close of that conversation

Promise Me

Out of all the noteworthy mistakes you've made
promise me you'll remember how much I adore you
The way you lean your head to the right when you're fishing
memories from the ocean of thoughts in your mind

How you awkwardly laugh when you are unsure what to do
The way you manage to keep a smile on your face when it seems
like the entire world is imploding

Promise me you'll remember no one else can leave your
fingerprints in this world
Firmly grab hold of as many hearts as you can
and mark them with the essence of your love

Unconditional

Promise me you'll remember...

About the Author

Estee E Dot Marie is a California raised Nigerian American with a passion for the arts. Her name Estee is French in origin meaning Star. Her goal is to be like a star and shine bright in the darkness. She has overcome some dark childhood trauma and looks to shine a light in the world that allows others to find internal peace and healing.

She began writing poetry in 8th-grade when she took a creative writing class. She fell in love with Edgar Allen Poe's writings first. Poetry became her therapy. Through her writing, she was able to express the feelings she never spoke. Maya Angelou is another author who has been a source of inspiration for her. As she matured she discovered spoken word and found another tool to her personal healing kit.

As a spoken word artist, she has taken her poetry to various churches in the greater Los Angeles area, Orange County, and beyond facilitating workshops and performing. She has been featured at the Flappers Comedy Club, The J-Spot, Gospel Rhythms Radio, Urban Soul Radio, Biola University, Verses LTE, What's Up With That with Pastor Michael Fisher, etc. She has produced spoken word events and has co-hosted a spoken word Television show, "SPEAK," which aired on Time Warner Cable's Faith On Demand channel. Her faith is an integral part of who she is and can be seen throughout this collection.

It is her goal to be a light in a dark world – to be a voice for those who have felt silenced, and to help children and adults unlock the creative expression that is on the inside of them.

www.ingramcontent.com/pod-product-compliance
Lightning Source LLC
Chambersburg PA
CBHW042129100526
44587CB00026B/4227